THIMBLEBERRY STORIES

Cynthia Rylant

ILLUSTRATED BY *Maggie Kneen*

HARCOURT, INC.

Printed in China

ISBN 10   0-15-356607-8
ISBN 13   978-0-15-356607-3

THIMBLEBERRY
STORIES

For Heather —C. R.

For Ella and Charlie Hitchman, with love —M. K.

CONTENTS

Nigel Meets Dipper

NIGEL CHIPMUNK LIVED IN A COZY LITTLE cottage on Thimbleberry Lane, and he was quite the homebody. Each morning he breakfasted on dandelion scones with lavender tea. Then he set about his housework. He had painted his house bright blue and each day gave it a nice scrubbing inside and out. He had even built himself a tiny gazebo for evening thinking, and of this he was particularly proud. He was a contented young fellow.

Nigel had grown up on Thimbleberry Lane and considered it quite the most beautiful place in the world. There were wild red roses growing all along the lane, and daylilies, and honeysuckle, and since it lay far out in the countryside, it was ever so quiet and peaceful. The animals who lived beside the lane were all very neighborly, and at night one could often find a little group of them at someone's home, sharing secrets, their laughter making the candlelight flicker in the dark.

Life did not change much from day to day on Thimbleberry Lane, but one morning something *did* change, and this was lucky for Nigel.

He was taking his morning stroll, wearing a bright yellow bowler hat and an indigo scarf, when he heard an unfamiliar voice behind a clutch of foxgloves. Nigel stopped and cocked his head lightly to one side.

"And a dash of this, a sprinkle of that, a fluff of the other," said a small voice.

Someone must be cooking, thought Nigel, though he could smell nothing delicious in the air.

He stepped to the side of the lane and carefully spread apart the foxgloves so he might see the puzzling chef.

But a chef he did not see. Instead, to his surprise, Nigel saw a new dwelling on Thimbleberry Lane. It was a tiny, funny little house. And all of it was round. The house was round, the windows were round, the front door was round. Over the door someone had written the word *Welcome.* But Nigel could not imagine many visitors fitting into such a round, miniature place. He himself would never fit. Why, he could not even put his head through the window to look in.

From inside the round house floated the voice again.

"A bit of here, a bit of there," it said. "Bits of lovely everywhere."

Nigel straightened his hat, cleared his throat, and called out, "Hello? Good morning! Anyone about?"

Quicker than Nigel could blink, a tiny head appeared in one of the windows.

"Yes, about I am!" someone said. And before Nigel could open his mouth to answer, the fellow had disappeared from the window and zipped out the front door.

It was a hummingbird! Why, Nigel had not seen a hummingbird on Thimbleberry Lane since he was a youngster. He'd heard they were all living in the poppy gardens at the Governor's mansion.

"How do you do," said Nigel gladly. "So nice to have a hummingbird move in."

"Thank you! I am Dipper, and as you can see, I am moved in and moved in for good."

As he spoke, the little hummingbird moved left to right, back to front, front to back, right to left so quickly Nigel was nearly made dizzy. He gave his head a shake to clear things up.

"My name is Nigel, and I thought you were cooking."

Dipper laughed and buzzed left to right.

"Oh no, not cooking. Haven't you noticed the paint all over me?"

Nigel blushed.

"I'm afraid you move so fast, I hardly see you at all."

"Oh dear," said Dipper cheerfully. He then hovered in place, his little wings humming steadily.

"Is this better?"

"Much!" answered Nigel, enjoying the new breeze.

"And now I see what you mean. What are you painting?"

"Oh my, everything. Would you care to come in for tea?"

Nigel looked at the tiny round door.

"I'm afraid I'm the wrong size for a hummingbird home."

Dipper laughed.

"Of course! Oh, I've been living in the poppy gardens too long. I've forgotten not all the world is hummingbirds. That is why I moved to Thimbleberry Lane: *variety.*

"Shall I bring my paintings out here then?" Dipper asked.

"Pardon me?" said Nigel. "I thought you were painting your house."

"Oh no," answered Dipper. "I'll never get around to that. Too much trouble. I keep my houses small so there's less to tend." (Nigel, who lived for tending, could not understand this at all.)

"Wait here," said Dipper.

Nigel was about to say all right, but before he did, Dipper had zipped into his house and back out again with something in his beak.

Nigel smiled. He was growing used to Dipper's flashy style.

The hummingbird hovered near a flat rock and began placing tiny squares on it.

"My paintings," Dipper said proudly.

Nigel peered at each little square. Never had he seen paintings so tiny. Tiny as sunflower seeds.

"Why, these are landscapes!" he said in surprise.

"Yes," answered Dipper.

"I thought you would paint small things," said Nigel.

"I live small but I see big," answered Dipper. "Do you like them?"

"They are extraordinary," said Nigel.

"Then they are yours," said Dipper, flying left to right and back and forth above them.

"I beg your pardon?" said Nigel.

"I paint all the time," said Dipper. "I've never been one to sit by the fire. I have many paintings and more to come. These are yours if you like."

"I am absolutely delighted!" answered Nigel. "You must return home with me. I'll fix supper for us and you can give me advice on where to hang them."

"Certainly," said Dipper. And before Nigel could, of

course, respond, the little hummingbird had gone inside and returned again, dressed for dinner.

"I hope you don't mind the paint on my nose," said Dipper. "It doesn't wash well."

"Not at all," said Nigel.

And together they returned to Nigel's dear blue cottage, where Nigel made a lovely meal of violet soup and rye toast and told Dipper all about life on Thimbleberry Lane.

Afterward, they hung paintings throughout the house.

And when Dipper had gone home in the evening, Nigel pulled a chair up to his favorite painting, and, taking out a magnifying glass, gazed at it all night long.

Little Owl Redecorates

NIGEL CHIPMUNK HAD MANY FRIENDS. There was Dipper, the hummingbird who lived down the lane. There was Mudpuppy, the salamander in Passalong Pond. Over in Moon Meadow were Claudius the garter snake and Copper the butterfly. And, of course, there was Little Owl, who lived all alone up in Haymaker Hollow.

Little Owl was fussy. He tried to be pleased by things, but he never quite was. In winter he wanted summer, in

summer he wanted spring. The apples were always a bit too tart and the cherries rather too soft. But he was a good-hearted owl, and a faithful friend, and for these qualities Nigel liked him very much.

One day, when Nigel was replacing a few of the broken bricks on his chimney, Little Owl came swooping through the air and landed beside him.

"Little Owl," said Nigel, "it is the middle of the day. Shouldn't you be asleep?"

Little Owl's feathers were standing straight up on his head, and his eyes were wide and he looked very much awake.

"I haven't slept for three days!" he said. "I'm redecorating. And I'm having a terrible time of it, Nigel. I've moved my bed twenty times already and it still isn't right."

Nigel looked more closely at Little Owl and saw the dark circles under his eyes.

"You have dark circles under your eyes, Little Owl," he said. "You really should sleep."

"Those are feathers, Nigel, feathers! We owls have dark circles! What I need isn't sleep. What I need is a friend to tell me where to put things. Will you come to my house and tell me where to put things?"

Nigel sighed. He really had hoped to finish the chimney this day. But Little Owl was in such a state.

"Of course," said Nigel. "Give me time to wash up and I'll be over by two o'clock."

"Righto," said Little Owl. He was very glad Nigel was coming. But too worried to smile. He gave a wave and flew home. Nigel went inside and poured some nice cool water into a basin, and scrubbed his face and

hands with a bar of peppermint soap. Then he donned a little red scarf and some sturdy black walkers and off he went.

Haymaker Hollow was in the hills northeast of Thimbleberry Lane. It was a straight-up walk, which could be pleasant in the cool of evening but at midday in summer quite a task. Nigel had forgotten to wear a hat against the sun, so he found a large plantain leaf and wrapped it about his head with a piece of corn silk. Luckily he didn't pass anyone along the way who might laugh at him. He passed only a porcupine, who never laughed at anybody because she herself always looked a little silly. (All those garish quills!)

When Nigel arrived at Little Owl's house, he found the bird leaning into a heavy sideboard and pushing it across the dining room.

"Little Owl!" exclaimed Nigel. "You are too small and feathery for such a job!" He rushed over to help his friend.

"Antiques," puffed Little Owl. "Can't help myself, I'm afraid. I know I should buy the lighter, more modern furniture. But I can't resist mahogany, you know."

"I know," grunted Nigel, guiding the sideboard against the wall with one final push.

"There," said Nigel. "Looks perfect."

Little Owl stepped back.

"Hmmm," he said, looking it over.

"Perfect," repeated Nigel with emphasis.

"Hmmm," said Little Owl.

While Little Owl was pondering, Nigel gazed about at all the rooms of the house. The whole place was a disaster: Furniture shifted and lopsided. Crockery and

knickknacks all about. Rugs rolled up and half-rolled and even a few out in the yard, obviously thrown through the window.

"Little Owl, you need to sleep," said Nigel.

"I think the sideboard should go *there*," said Little Owl, pointing to the other side of the room, which presently held an old Victrola. The bird's eyes were wild and shiny.

"Let me fix you a cup of warm milk," said Nigel, leading his friend to an old leather armchair that had been temporarily shoved into a closet.

"And that angel statue," said Little Owl, pointing, "should go *there*."

"In time, in time," answered Nigel, patting his friend's shoulder. "Just relax."

The chipmunk had no trouble locating the milk,

though finding Little Owl's stove was a challenge. But soon Nigel had two steaming mugs in hand.

He found a velvet hassock and sat near Little Owl, who was still surveying his house, his owl head spinning nearly completely around.

"Oh-oh-oh," whispered Little Owl. He was no good with chaos. No good at all.

"Little Owl, where was your sideboard before?" asked Nigel, sipping his milk.

Little Owl pointed.

"And your chaise?"

Little Owl pointed again.

"And where was the grand piano?"

Nigel continued asking where all of the furniture had been in the first place, and Little Owl pointed.

"And how did you like the furniture where it was before?" asked Nigel.

"Oh, quite well. Quite well, indeed," said Little Owl, taking a drink of his milk, then trying to smooth down the feathers on top of his head. "It took me years to make it all work."

"Well then, *why* did you want to shift everything about?" asked Nigel.

"Because of the gladiola," answered Little Owl matter-of-factly.

"What gladiola?" asked Nigel.

"That one there," said Little Owl, pointing.

Nigel looked across the parlor and across the dining room and across the kitchen to a small window beside the back door. On the sill was a glass jar, and in the glass jar was a gladiola.

"And what's wrong with the gladiola?" asked Nigel.

"Nothing," said Little Owl. "But it's pink. And the only pink thing in my house is the French floor lamp. So I moved it into the kitchen, nearer the gladiola. To coordinate, you know. But then the Windsor chair didn't look quite right without the lamp. So I moved that. Then the hat rack didn't look right, so I moved that, too. And the next thing I knew, my furniture was everywhere and my feathers were sticking straight up on my head and I was sitting on your chimney in a daze!"

Nigel smiled. He thought a bit.

"Little Owl," he said presently, "I like gladiolas very much. Would it trouble you to let me have that pink one to take home?"

"But of course you may have it," said Little Owl. "You are my dear friend."

"Then let us set it out by the gate so I won't forget it. Then we will redecorate."

"Certainly," said Little Owl, whose manners were always impeccable. He carried the glass jar with the flower out to the gate and left it there for his friend.

When he walked back into his house, Little Owl looked around and said suddenly, "Of course! The side-board goes *there*!"

Nigel helped him push it.

"Perfect!" said Little Owl. "Now, the grand piano goes *here!*"

Nigel helped him push that, too.

"Perfect!" cried Little Owl.

Nigel helped Little Owl push all the furniture back where it had been before. They returned all the knick-knacks to their proper places and rolled each rug into its perfect position on the floor.

When they were finished, Nigel took his pink gladiola and walked back home. It was evening now. He didn't need a plantain hat.

He carried the gladiola near his nose, to breathe its lovely fragrance, and as he walked he admired the moon and the stars in the sky.

Nigel had a very good sleep that night. And his friend Little Owl had an even better one. He slept for four days.

But when finally Little Owl awoke, he flew first thing to see his friend Nigel, with whom he had cinnamon tea and raspberry buns and a good laugh about all that furniture.

Claudius Plants a Garden

J UST TO THE EAST OF THIMBLEBERRY LANE lay Moon Meadow. The meadow was wide and flat and full of weeds and wildflowers, making it a perfect place for small snakes and butterflies. Nigel Chipmunk often walked over from Thimbleberry Lane to visit his good friends Claudius and Copper in the meadow. Claudius was a friendly brown garter snake with an impressive yellow stripe along his back. Copper was a swallowtail butterfly with profound gold and blue

markings. Nigel considered them his two most decorative friends.

One day when he was feeling restless after finishing up the laundry and tidying the little blue cottage he loved so well, Nigel decided to take a trip over to Moon Meadow to see his friends. Being a thoughtful chipmunk, he looked for something to bring them. Out in his garden the strawberries were plump and red. Perfect for two fine hosts. Nigel put three berries into a small tin pail and set out east.

One always knows when one has arrived at Moon Meadow, for it is where Thimbleberry Lane ends—or begins, depending on how one looks at it. Nigel walked along the lane until he was stopped by a tall shock of weeds three feet high, and this, he knew, was the meadow's edge. He gingerly stepped into the thick grasses and carefully made his way southeast toward Copper's house.

Claudius would likely be there, as well. Though he had his own home, Claudius preferred Copper's house. It was quite colorful and very different from his own drab brown one. The windows were trimmed with cur-tains of bold red and yellow and black. The sofa was bright green. The kitchen table purple. Copper herself was very colorful, too. She often went about the house with a fantastic shawl draped across her shoulders and ornaments hanging from her antennae. Nearly every day Claudius could be found visiting, stretched upon the bright green sofa or wrapped around the porch swing (which was an electric blue).

Nigel Chipmunk made his way through the tall grasses and, as expected, when he arrived both Copper and Claudius were there, playing a game of backgammon on the front steps.

"Nigel!" they called at once. Copper tossed back her shawl and fluttered her wings in delight. Claudius stood on the tip of his tail, swaying back and forth in a dance. Nigel greeted them with the enthusiasm of a friend long unseen.

The three then moved into the kitchen and gathered around the purple table for glasses of iced rose nectar. Ever the colorful hostess, Copper put a long stem of sweet pea into each glass.

"I've brought strawberries, as you can see," said Nigel. "You must try them. They're quite delicious."

"I don't believe I've eaten strawberries before," said Claudius, putting on his eyeglasses for a better look. (Copper had brought out tiny moon-shaped saucers and was cutting the berries into small bites for each of them.)

"Never eaten strawberries?" said Nigel.

"We don't have them here in the meadow. Too many weeds," answered Claudius. "And of course I am much too long and lazy to go off to market to buy any. I can live on beetles quite well, with Copper's fine nectar to wash them down."

Copper smiled.

"Fifty-two flavors to choose from," she said. "And today a chestnut tart for dessert."

"Lovely," said Nigel. "Here, do try the strawberries, Claudius. I believe you'll like them."

Pushing his eyeglasses to the top of his head, Claudius gracefully leaned over the saucer and delicately plucked a piece of strawberry with his teeth.

He chewed a moment. Nigel waited.

A slow, wide smile spread across the snake's face.

"Oh my," he said smoothly. "Oh my, oh my, oh my." And he plucked another.

Nigel, Claudius, and Copper had a lovely lunch of nectar, strawberries, and chestnut tart. Afterward they sat in the parlor sipping hollyhock tea.

Claudius, feeling quite dreamy and content, said to Nigel, "Do you think, Nigel, I might grow strawberries of my own?"

Nigel set down his teacup.

"Why, of course, Claudius. Anyone may grow straw-berries if he is willing to try."

"I am so lazy, you know," answered Claudius. "But for those juicy wonders, I believe you could get even me to take up a hoe."

"I'll bring you some seedlings on Friday," said Nigel.

And as he promised, Nigel Chipmunk pulled on his gardening gloves and pushed a small wheelbarrow full of strawberry seedlings and good soil to Claudius's house on Friday.

The snake had pulled some pieces of an old foot-bridge into his yard to make a little raised bed for the plants, and he was coiled in the middle of it, napping, when Nigel arrived.

"Claudius!" called Nigel as he approached.

"Hmmm?" said the sleepy snake.

"I'm very proud of you, Claudius! You did make a strawberry bed!"

"*Bed* is exactly the right word," said the yawning snake as he pulled himself up for work.

"Let's get started," said Nigel, picking up a plant.

Together the two friends spread the good soil into the raised bed, then as Nigel dug small holes, Claudius popped plants into them. Claudius had borrowed one of Copper's magenta sunbonnets for the day, and he looked quite the gardener.

After all of the plants were in and watered, Nigel and Claudius went into the kitchen for a cold drink.

"I'm afraid I have only water," apologized the snake. "I live such a bachelor's life."

"Water is perfect," said Nigel, taking a paper cup from Claudius.

"I hate washing dishes," the snake explained. "Paper cups, water, and a can or two of beetles are, I'm afraid, all you will find."

Nigel, who loved cooking and real china cups and a larder stocked with food, simply smiled.

"What makes it all a feast," he said, "is the fine company."

This made Claudius very glad.

Nigel, of course, did not really expect any of the strawberry plants to grow. His long and lazy friend would probably neither weed nor water the garden. Nigel had helped Claudius plant the seedlings simply because the idea seemed to make the snake so happy. But Nigel had little hope of any ripe berries.

Thus he was surprised and delighted when one evening Copper and Claudius appeared at his door carrying an enormous strawberry pie.

"Picked the berries myself," Claudius said with a grin.

Happily, Nigel spread his table with a sunflower cloth and his best china saucers, and the three had a luxurious strawberry feast. Claudius took credit for the

tasty strawberries all through the meal. Then finally, with tea, he laughingly admitted that really his garden had failed and he'd bought the berries at market.

"But I did pick them off the produce shelf myself!" the snake said proudly.

Nigel pretended to be surprised at the joke and pleased with Claudius's silly trick.

But in truth, Nigel had known all along, for earlier he had eaten a three-cents sticker off one of the berries!

But he never told.

Mudpuppy's Picnic

WHEN HE WAS NOT BUSY TENDING HIS little blue cottage on Thimbleberry Lane, Nigel Chipmunk often liked to walk down to Passalong Pond, where his friend Mudpuppy lived. Mudpuppy was a stout, gray salamander who was always trying to improve himself. He did leg-lifts each morning, ate only the worst-tasting foods because he thought they were better for him, and even one summer tried to read every book in the Thimbleberry Library so he might become a more interesting salamander. In spite of Mudpuppy's attempts at perfection, Nigel very much enjoyed his company, especially since Mudpuppy was such a good boatman.

Nigel loved to boat, but he wasn't very good at it. When once he built his own little rowboat to take out on Passalong Pond, he wound up living on water bugs for two days because he could not get the boat to make a straight line back to shore. But this did not dampen Nigel's enthusiasm for boating—so long as someone else was navigating. And in this role Mudpuppy, being a pond dweller, was superb.

Thus one hot summer day when Nigel was weary of ground and grass, he decided to visit Mudpuppy in hopes of boating.

Naturally the salamander was delighted to see him.

Mudpuppy was in his kitchen concocting a health tonic when Nigel arrived. The tonic must have consisted of a good number of beets, for there were slippery purple puddles everywhere. Mudpuppy offered Nigel a drink of tonic—"to stiffen the spine and ankles," he said—and being a considerate chipmunk, Nigel accepted, though he was not much interested either in tonics or spines. As expected, the drink was quite nasty, but Nigel drank it as delicately as he could and promised himself next time to bring his own refreshments to Passalong Pond.

"Would you care to go boating today?" Nigel asked his friend.

"Yes, indeed!" answered the salamander. "Swimming alone gets so tiresome. It will be lovely to have a companion on the pond. Fresh air, sun—nothing better for the health!" Nigel, who was actually more interested in *floating*, politely agreed.

"And shall I pack us a picnic lunch to take?" asked Mudpuppy.

Nigel hesitated. Although he very much disliked Mudpuppy's food, he could think of no way out of the situation. Mudpuppy might be offended if he said no thank you, so instead Nigel said, "Lovely."

"Excellent!" said Mudpuppy. "Why don't you run

out to the dock then and ready the boat, while I put a few things together here. And I see you've no boating hat. Take one of mine. I'll be out in a wink."

Nigel accepted the hat and Mudpuppy's kindness with gratitude. The salamander's good heart more than made up for the bad taste of his tonics.

Nigel went out toward the dock, eagerly approaching Mudpuppy's boat. There she was, a lovely birch boat that Mudpuppy had christened "Fern." Nigel set about brushing leaves from Fern's interior, checking the condition of her oars, wiping a bit of mud from her prow. The boat bobbed gently up and down in the water, and for a moment Nigel remembered the thrill of having his own little boat, being his own sailor. Then he remembered the water bugs and was glad he'd given the boat to a beaver and her babies on the other side of the pond.

Presently Mudpuppy arrived, a large green knapsack slung across his back. Nigel dreaded to think what sort of lunch might be inside that pack. He decided to put it out of his mind and enjoy the day.

With Mudpuppy at the oars, Nigel untied the boat, giving it a good push from the dock, and they were off. The coolness of the breeze, the green silvery water, the clear blue sky . . . all these made Nigel wonder why he had not been born a salamander.

Mudpuppy always kept a net in the boat for entertainment, and he and Nigel amused themselves by seeing what they could scoop up. First they scooped a crayfish, who gave them a good piece of her mind before returning to the water. Then they scooped a cricket frog, who was quite relieved it was only a salamander and chipmunk who had netted him and not a little boy who

might take him home to live in a jar. And they scooped more water bugs than either cared to count.

Tired from all the excitement of scooping, they lay back in the boat and let it lead itself as they talked of the goings-on in Passalong Pond and on Thimbleberry Lane. Nigel told Mudpuppy about the new brick floor he was putting in his kitchen, and the salamander had some very useful advice for making the bricks stick. They talked easily and quietly, as friends do when floating on water on a beautiful day. Then Mudpuppy announced it was lunchtime.

Oh dear, thought Nigel, and though his stomach was feeling very empty, he could not bring himself to look forward to the meal. Still, he managed an enthusiastic response and helped Mudpuppy pull up at a small shaded island on the pond. The two found a nice soft spot free of pine needles, and Mudpuppy brought forth the pack.

First the salamander carefully removed a lovely picnic cloth of blue-and-white check. Then he brought out sparkling pink crockery plates and real crystal goblets and silver flatware. Nigel was amazed. He had never seen a picnic so beautifully prepared. He told himself that no matter how nasty the food might be, the tableware would more than make up for the lack of such things as potato salad and deviled eggs.

And just as Nigel was thinking this, Mudpuppy took the cover off of a crockery pot and revealed to him a lovely yellow potato salad! Then a lid came off a platter of cold deviled eggs decorated with olives! And to Nigel's further astonishment, Mudpuppy unveiled the crowning touch: a two-layer chocolate cake!

"But Mudpuppy—how did you ever manage all this in so short a time?" asked Nigel.

The salamander smiled.

"Since our last meal together, when you turned quite green over the broccoli-beet salad, I determined to always have something better to prepare for your next visit, dear friend. Enjoy!"

The salamander then pulled forth a large, brown sandwich bursting with turnip mash and bean curd for himself. He bit into the sandwich with gusto.

It was the most magnificent picnic Nigel had ever attended. And to repay Mudpuppy for his extraordinary kindness, at day's end Nigel himself rowed them all the way back home.

And in a perfectly straight line!